THE SEXUAL INTELLECTUAL

Edited by
Dave Pandres, Jr.

Illustrated by
Roger Lozano

LONGSTREET PRESS
Atlanta, Georgia

Published by
LONGSTREET PRESS, INC.
2150 Newmarket Parkway
Suite 102
Marietta, Georgia 30067

Text © 1990 by Dave Pandres, Jr.
Illustrations © 1990 by Roger Lozano

All rights reserved. No part of this book may be reproduced in any form or by any means without the prior written permission of the Publisher, excepting brief quotes used in connection with reviews, written specifically for inclusion in a magazine or newspaper.

Printed in the United States of America
93 92 91 90   5 4 3 2 1

Library of Congress Catalog Card Number: 89-063794

ISBN 0-929264-74-6

Cover illustration by Gary Weiss

FOREWORD

My original plan was to present these quotations in chronological order because I recalled some very humorous Biblical passages, such as a line in the *Old Testament* which describes Abraham's posterior as the most elastic object in the world:

Abraham tied his ass to a tree and walked twenty miles in every direction.

Unfortunately, my memory was imprecise. The line is not Biblical but rather is due to the most prolific of all writers, a person named *Anonymous*. Indeed, my research showed that Biblical humor was concerned primarily with such matters as eyes for eyes and teeth for teeth. Except for the *Old Testament,* the earliest sexual humor I found was due to *Hipponax (c. 570-520 B.C.),* who stated that

There are two days when a woman is a pleasure: the day one marries her and the day one buries her.

When my wife failed to appreciate the humor in this, I briefly considered a presentation in reverse chronological order since modern writers have generally regarded women more favorably than did the ancients. I decided, however, that sex is a disorderly activity which deserves a disorderly presentation. That is what the reader will find in these pages. I then began to consider how I could guard against the evils of male chauvinism in selecting quotations for inclusion. I finally decided that this would present no problem because of my innate fair-mindedness and lack of any macho inclinations—although I did recall an occasion when my wife presented me with the gift of a beautiful tietack in the form of a male chauvinist pig.

The quotable writers include so many more males than females, however, that I believe it is appropriate to present in this Foreword the following quotation from Gail Sheehy, which is (I hope) the only serious one in the entire volume:

> If women had wives to keep house for them, to stay home with vomiting children, to get the car fixed, fight with the painters, run to the supermarket, reconcile the bank statements, listen to everyone's problems, cater the dinner parties, and nourish the spirit each night, just imagine the possibilities for expansion—the number of books that would be written, companies started, professorships filled, political offices that would be held, by women.

It is quite possible that I have gilded the lily by including this statement from Ms. Sheehy because the smaller number of women quoted are more than a match for the larger number of men. I would hate to meet one of these ladies in a dark alley if she was armed with a word processor.

— DAVE PANDRES, JR.

THE SEXUAL INTELLECTUAL™

SEXUAL INTELLECTUAL

> *Kissing is a means of getting two people so close together that they can't see anything wrong with each other.*
> — René Yasenek

> *When it comes to broken marriages, most husbands will split the blame — half his wife's fault and half her mother's.*
> — Anonymous

In Biblical times a man could have as many wives as he could afford. Just like today.
— *Abigail Van Buren*

SEXUAL INTELLECTUAL

It must be admitted that we English have sex on the brain, which is a very unfortunate place to have it.
— *Malcolm Muggeridge*

Sex is good, but not as good as fresh sweet corn.
— *Garrison Keillor*

Sex drive: a physical craving that begins in adolescence and ends at marriage.
— *Robert Byrne*

Guns don't kill people; husbands that come home early kill people.
— *Don Rose*

I do not know if she was virtuous, but she was ugly, and with a woman that is half the battle.
— *Heinrich Heine*

SEXUAL INTELLECTUAL

An Irishman is the only man in the world who will step over the bodies of a dozen naked women to get to a bottle of stout.
— *Anonymous*

There will be sex after death; we just won't be able to feel it.
— *Lily Tomlin*

I hated my marriage, but I always had a great place to park.
— *Gerald Nachman*

The girl who remembers her first kiss now has a daughter who can't even remember her first husband.
— *Anonymous*

SEXUAL INTELLECTUAL

American women expect to find in their husbands a perfection that English women only hope to find in their butlers.

— *W. Somerset Maugham*

SEXUAL INTELLECTUAL

If men acted after marriage as they do during courtship, there would be fewer divorces — and more bankruptcies.
— *Frances Rodman*

> The trouble with wedlock is there's not enough wed and too much lock.
> — *Christopher Morley*

A man usually falls in love with a woman who asks the kinds of questions he is able to answer.
— *Ronald Coleman*

SEXUAL INTELLECTUAL

Lord, make me chaste . . . but not yet.
— *St. Augustine*

Love is the delightful interval between meeting a beautiful girl and discovering that she looks like a haddock.
— *John Barrymore*

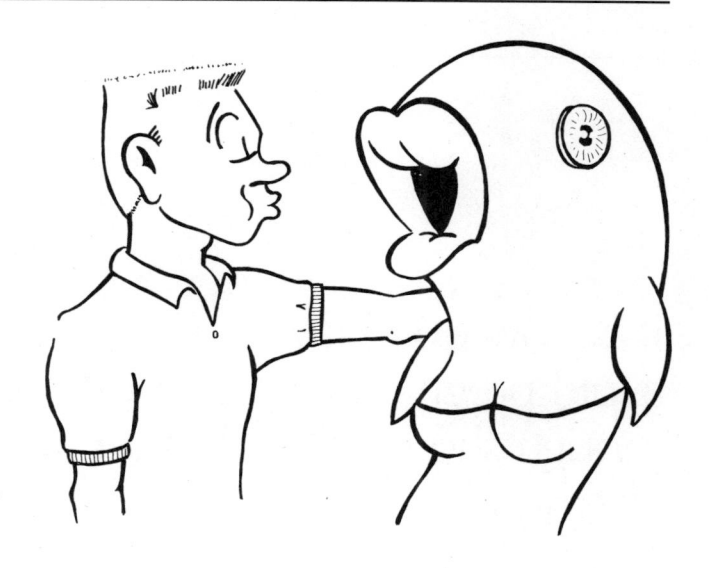

SEXUAL INTELLECTUAL

> *When I'm good I'm very, very good, but when I'm bad I'm better.*
> — Mae West

Being a woman is of special interest to aspiring male transsexuals. To actual women, it is simply a good excuse not to play football.
— Fran Lebowitz

It is now quite lawful for a Catholic woman to avoid pregnancy by a resort to mathematics, though she is still forbidden to resort to physics or chemistry.
— H. L. Mencken

SEXUAL INTELLECTUAL

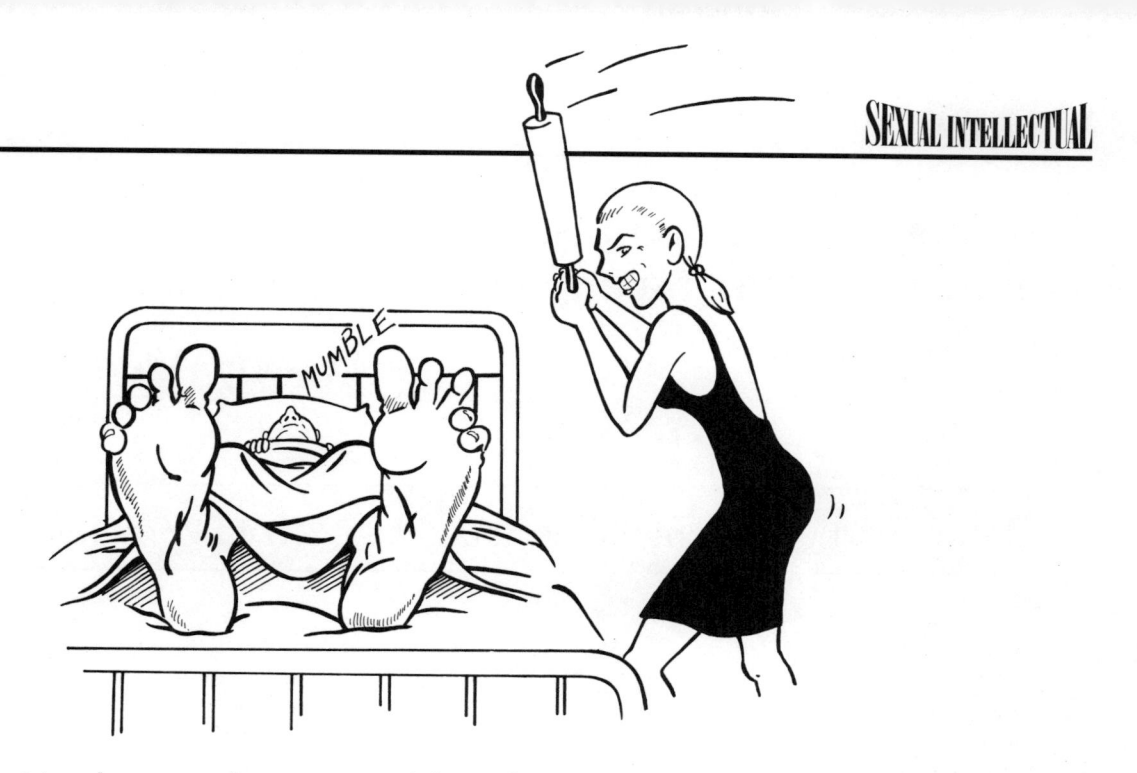

You have only to mumble a few words in church to get married and a few words in your sleep to get divorced.
— *Anonymous*

SEXUAL INTELLECTUAL

The difference between sex and death is, with death you can do it alone and nobody's going to make fun of you.
— *Woody Allen*

> Platonic love is from the neck up. — *Thyra Winslow*

A teenage girl is a pert glance, a sparkling smile, a twinkle in the eye, a twinkle in the pants and a real hard thing to explain to your wife.
— *P.J. O'Rourke*

Women who seek to be equal to men lack ambition.
— *Timothy Leary*

Eunuch: a man who has had his works cut out for him.
— *Robert Byrne*

SEXUAL INTELLECTUAL

> *All women's dresses are merely variations on the eternal struggle between the admitted desire to dress and the unadmitted desire to undress.*
> — Lin Yutang

> *God created man and, finding him not sufficiently alone, gave him a companion to make him feel his solitude more keenly.*
> — Paul Valéry

If you are living with a man, you don't have to worry about whether you should sleep with him after dinner.
— *Stephanie Brush*

Any married man should forget his mistakes. No use in two people remembering the same thing.
— *Duane Dewel*

From birth to age eighteen, a girl needs good parents. From eighteen to thirty-five, she needs good looks. From thirty-five to fifty-five, she needs a good personality. From fifty-five on, she needs good cash.
— Sophie Tucker

Bed is the poor man's opera.
— Italian proverb

SEXUAL INTELLECTUAL

All husbands are alike, but they have different faces so you can tell them apart.
— *Anonymous*

It's been so long since I made love I can't even remember who gets tied up. — *Joan Rivers*

SEXUAL INTELLECTUAL

Women are quite unlike men. Women have higher voices, longer hair, smaller waistlines, daintier feet and prettier hands. They also invariably have the upper hand.
— *Stephen Potter*

If you aren't going all the way, why go at all?
— Joe Namath

If a woman hasn't got a tiny streak of a harlot in her, she's dry as a stick as a rule.
— D. H. Lawrence

SEXUAL INTELLECTUAL

To be in love is merely to be in a state of perpetual anesthesia — to mistake an ordinary young man for a Greek god or an ordinary young woman for a goddess.

— *H. L. Mencken*

Music played at weddings always reminds me of the music played for soldiers before they go into battle.

— *Heinrich Heine*

It doesn't much signify whom one marries, for one is sure to find the next morning that it was someone else.

— *Samuel Rogers*

SEXUAL INTELLECTUAL

I'm tired of all this business about beauty being only skin deep. That's deep enough. What do you want — an adorable pancreas?
— *Jean Kerr*

A man is only as old as the woman he feels.
— *Groucho Marx*

SEXUAL INTELLECTUAL

A liberated woman is one who has sex before marriage and a job after.
 — Gloria Steinem

The conception of two people living together for twenty-five years without having a cross word suggests a lack of spirit only to be admired in sheep.
 — Sir Alan Patrick Herbert

I'd rather be black than gay because when you're black you don't have to tell your mother.
 — *Charles Pierce*

Bachelors know more about women than married men; if they didn't, they'd be married too.
— *H.L. Mencken*

If you want to read about love and marriage, you've got to buy two separate books.
— *Alan King*

The most romantic thing any woman ever said to me in bed was, "Are you sure you're not a cop?"
— *Larry Brown*

Sexual Intellectual

Somewhere on this globe, every ten seconds, there is a woman giving birth to a child. She must be found and stopped.
— *Sam Levinson*

Marriage is like a bank account. You put it in, you take it out, you lose interest.
— *Professor Irwin Corey*

> *In nine cases out of ten, a woman had better show more affection than she feels.*
> — Jane Austen

I'm not denyin' the women are foolish; God Almighty made 'em to match the men.
— *George Eliot*

Wives are usually their husband's mental inferiors and spiritual superiors; this gives them double instruments of torture.
— *Don Herold*

Sexual intellectual

> *When a woman marries again, it is because she detested her first husband. When a man marries again, it is because he adored his first wife. Women try their luck; men risk theirs.*
> — Oscar Wilde

> *Men are always doomed to be duped, not so much by the arts of the [other] sex as by their own imaginations. They are always wooing goddesses and marrying mere mortals.*
> — Washington Irving

Some husbands are living proof that a woman can take a joke. — *Anonymous*

SEXUAL INTELLECTUAL

Bachelors should be heavily taxed. It is not fair that some men should be happier than others.
— *Oscar Wilde*

When women kiss, it always reminds me of prizefighters shaking hands.
— *H. L. Mencken*

SEXUAL INTELLECTUAL

Marriage is one long conversation checkered by disputes.
— *Robert Louis Stevenson*

> *If I had been the Virgin Mary, I would have said, "No."*
> — Stevie Smith

A woman is the only thing I am afraid of that I know will not hurt me.
— *Abraham Lincoln*

SEXUAL INTELLECTUAL

Women's intuition is the result of millions of years of not thinking.
— *Rupert Hughes*

After we made love, he took a piece of chalk and made an outline of my body.
— *Joan Rivers*

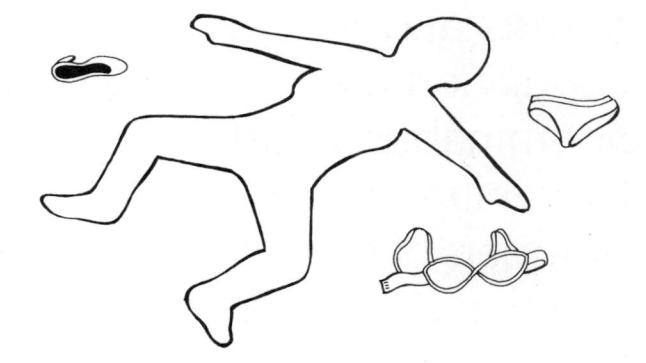

SEXUAL INTELLECTUAL

When a girl marries, she exchanges the attentions of many men for the inattention of one.
— *Helen Rowland*

Mirrors and copulation are abominable because they increase the numbers of men.
— *Jorge Luis Borges*

> *I find that my wife hath something in her gizzard that only waits an opportunity of being provoked to bring up; but I will not, for my content-sake, give it.*
> — Samuel Pepys

SEXUAL INTELLECTUAL

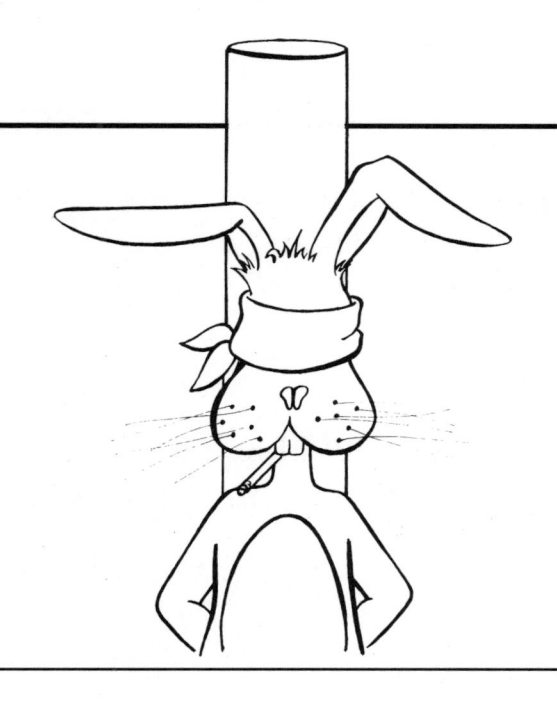

Some men are so macho they'll get you pregnant just to kill a rabbit.
— *Maureen Murphy*

A promiscuous person is usually someone who is getting more sex than you are.
— *Victor Lownes*

SEXUAL INTELLECTUAL

Many a man owes his success to his first wife and his second wife to his success.

— *Jim Backus*

A diplomatic husband's apology to his wife: How do you expect me to remember your birthday when you never look any older?

— *Anonymous*

A single sentence will suffice for modern man: He fornicated and read the papers.

— *Albert Camus*

It was not the apple on the tree, but the pair on the ground, I believe, that caused the trouble in the garden.
— M.D. O'Connor

Among the porcupines, rape is unknown.
— *Gregory Clark*

A father's business advice to his son: Go into ladies' lingerie. There will always be room in panties and brassieres for a young man with a little cash and a lot of imagination.
— *Anonymous*

SEXUAL INTELLECTUAL

She cried, and the judge wiped her tears on my checkbook.
— *Tommy Manville*

Marriage is the price men pay for sex; sex is the price women pay for marriage.
— *Anonymous*

I used to be a virgin, but I gave it up because there was no money in it.
— *Marsha Warfield*

The person who marries for money usually earns every penny of it.
— *Anonymous*

The trouble with living in sin is the shortage of closet space.
— *Missy Dizick*

SEXUAL INTELLECTUAL

All this fuss about sleeping together. For physical pleasure I'd sooner go to my dentist any day.
— *Evelyn Waugh*

> *Whoever named it "necking" was a poor judge of anatomy.*
> — Groucho Marx

> *Marriage is neither heaven nor hell; it is simply purgatory.*
> — Abraham Lincoln

Before marriage the three little words are, "I love you." After marriage they are, "Let's eat out."
— *Anonymous*

SEXUAL INTELLECTUAL

Alimony is like buying oats for a dead horse.
— *Arthur Baer*

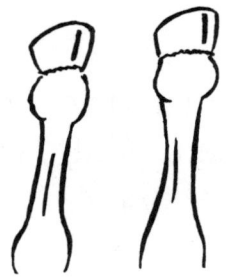

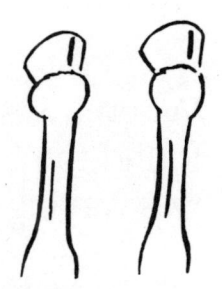

SEXUAL INTELLECTUAL

I never married because I have three pets at home that answer the same purpose as a husband. I have a dog that growls every morning, a parrot that swears all afternoon, and a cat that comes home late at night.
— Marie Corelli

> *Celibacy is not hereditary.*
> — Guy Goden

When I was a young man, I vowed never to marry until I found the ideal woman. Well, I found her — but, alas, she was waiting for the ideal man.
— Robert Schuman

SEXUAL INTELLECTUAL

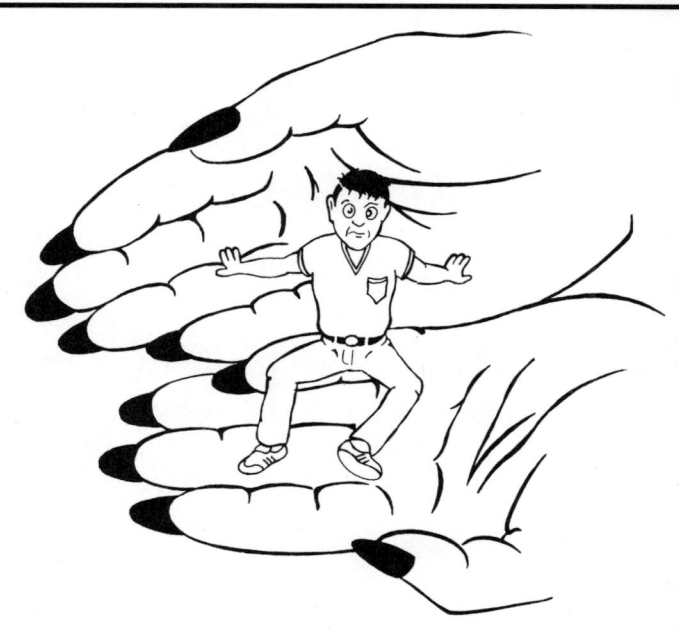

Woman would be more charming if one could fall into her arms without falling into her hands.
— *Ambrose Bierce*

Sexual Intellectual

We don't believe in rheumatism and true love until after the first attack.
— *Marie Ebner von Eschenbach*

My schoolmates would make love to anything that moved, but I never saw any reason to limit myself.
— *Emo Philips*

I refuse to consign the whole male sex to the nursery. I insist on believing that some men are my equals.
— *Brigid Brophy*

To my embarrassment I was born in bed with a lady.
— Wilson Mizner

If it weren't for pickpockets, I'd have no sex life at all.
— Rodney Dangerfield

A Roman divorced from his wife, being highly blamed by his friends, who demanded, "Was she not chaste? Was she not fair? Was she not fruitful?" holding out his shoe, asked them whether it was not new and well made. "Yet," added he, "none of you can tell me where it pinches me."
— *Plutarch*

SEXUAL INTELLECTUAL

Women sometimes forgive a man who forces the opportunity, but never a man who misses one.
— *Charles Maurice de Talleyrand-Perigord*

I wouldn't trust my husband with a young woman for five minutes, and he's been dead for twenty-five years.
— *Kathleen Kearney Behan*

I expect that Woman will be the last thing civilized by Man.
— *George Meredith*

SEXUAL INTELLECTUAL

The perfect lover is one who turns into a pizza at 4 A.M.
— *Charles Pierce*

SEXUAL INTELLECTUAL

Ever since the young men have owned motorcycles, incest has been dying out.
— *Max Frisch*

> *I wasn't kissing her; I was whispering in her mouth.*
> *— Chico Marx*

The most popular labor-saving device is still a husband with money.
— *Joey Adams*

SEXUAL INTELLECTUAL

The only people who make love all the time are liars.
— *Louis Jordan*

A husband is what is left of the lover after the nerve has been extracted.
— *Helen Rowland*

The orgasm has replaced the Cross as the focus of longing and image of fulfillment.
— *Malcolm Muggeridge*

How did sex come to be thought of as dirty in the first place? God must have been a Republican.
— *Will Durst*

SEXUAL INTELLECTUAL

When a woman gets married, it's like jumping into a hole in the ice in the middle of winter; you do it only once and you remember it for the rest of your days.
— *Maxim Gorky*

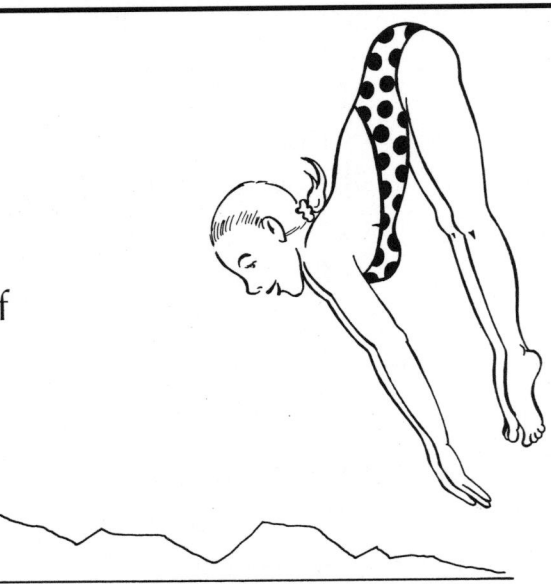

SEXUAL INTELLECTUAL

When two people are under the influence of the most violent, most insane, most delusive and most transient of passions, they are required to swear that they will remain in that excited, abnormal and exhausting condition continuously until death do them part.
— *George Bernard Shaw*

The average girl would rather have beauty than brains because she knows that the average man can see much better than he can think.
— *Anonymous*

I like young girls. Their stories are shorter.
— *Thomas McGuane*

SEXUAL INTELLECTUAL

When turkeys mate they think of swans.
— *Johnny Carson*

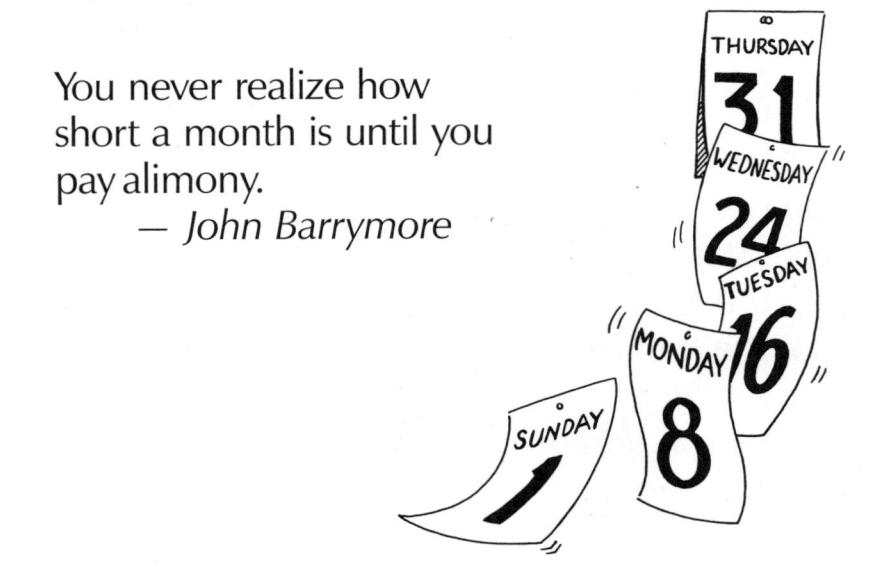

You never realize how short a month is until you pay alimony.
— *John Barrymore*

Whatever women do they must do twice as well as men to be thought half as good. Luckily, this is not difficult.
— *Charlotte Whitton*

> *The most difficult years of marriage are those following the wedding.*
> — Anonymous

Drying a widow's tears is one of the most dangerous occupations known to man.
— *Dorothy Dix*

SEXUAL INTELLECTUAL

> *Filth and old age, I'm sure you will agree, Are powerful wardens upon chastity.*
> — Geoffrey Chaucer

I'd like to get married because I like the idea of a man being required by law to sleep with me every night.
— *Carrie Snow*

My advice to the women's clubs of America is to raise more hell and fewer dahlias.
— *William Allen White*

SEXUAL INTELLECTUAL

To err is human, to forgive supine.
— S.J. Perelman

> *If you resolve to give up smoking, drinking and loving, you don't actually live longer . . . it just seems longer.*
> — Clement Freud

> *I believe a little incompatibility is the spice of life, particularly if he has income and she is pattable.*
> — Ogden Nash

I used to be Snow White . . . but I drifted.
— Mae West

SEXUAL INTELLECTUAL

Last time I tried to make love to my wife nothing was happening, so I said to her, "What's the matter, you can't think of anybody either?"
— *Rodney Dangerfield*

Love is being stupid together.
— *Paul Valéry*

SEXUAL INTELLECTUAL

Thank God for single people. America would never have been discovered if Christopher Columbus had been married: "You're going where? With whom? To find what? And I suppose she's giving you those ships for nothing?"
— *Richard Chamberlain*

> *Never play leapfrog with a unicorn.*
> — **Anonymous**

What a pity it is that nobody knows how to manage a wife but a bachelor.
— *George Coleman*

SEXUAL INTELLECTUAL

By all means marry: If you get a good wife, you'll become happy; if you get a bad one, you'll become a philosopher.
— *Socrates*

It is more fun contemplating someone else's navel than your own.
— *Arthur Hoppe*

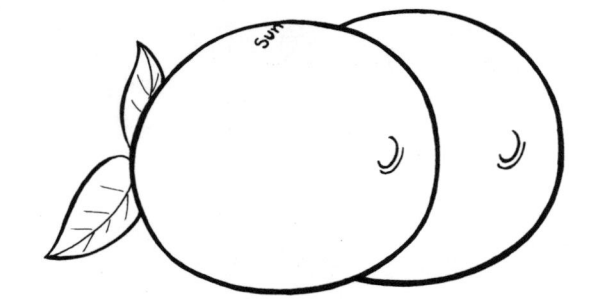

SEXUAL INTELLECTUAL

> I've tried several varieties of sex. The conventional position makes me claustrophobic, and the others give me a stiff neck or lockjaw.
> — Tallulah Bankhead

> Marriage is not merely sharing the fettucini but sharing the burden of finding the fettucini restaurant in the first place.
> — Calvin Trillin

Sex is the great amateur art. The professional, male or female, is frowned on; he or she misses the whole point and spoils the show.
— *David Cort*

Sexual Intellectual

Literature is mostly about having sex and not much about having children. Life is the other way around.

— *David Lodge*

Describing his own bald head: a solar panel on a sex machine.
— *Senator Alan Simpson*

If homosexuality were normal, God would have created Adam and Bruce.
— *Anita Bryant*

Absence makes the heart grow fonder — of someone else.
— *Anonymous*

I will find you twenty lascivious turtles ere one chaste man.
— *William Shakespeare*

Sexual Intellectual

A woman's like an elephant — I like to look at 'em, but I wouldn't want to own one!
— W. C. Fields

I'm a marvelous housekeeper. Everytime I leave a man I keep his house.
— Zsa Zsa Gabor

SEXUAL INTELLECTUAL

A man can sleep around, no questions asked, but if a woman makes nineteen or twenty mistakes she's a tramp.
— *Joan Rivers*

Alimony: the cash surrender value of a husband.
— Anonymous

Marriage is based on the theory that when a man discovers a particular brand of beer exactly to his taste he should at once throw up his job and go to work in the brewery.
— *George Jean Nathan*

SEXUAL INTELLECTUAL

Only two things are necessary to keep one's wife happy. One is let her think she is having her way and the other, to let her have it.
— *Lyndon Baines Johnson*

Mothers are fonder than fathers of their children because they are more certain they are their own.
— Aristotle

He and I had an office so tiny that an inch smaller and it would have been adultery.
— Dorothy Parker

SEXUAL INTELLECTUAL

Marriage has driven more than one man to sex.
— *Peter De Vries*

Women speak because they wish to speak, whereas a man speaks only when driven to speech by something outside himself — like, for instance, he can't find any clean socks.
— *Jean Kerr*

SEXUAL INTELLECTUAL

My mother-in-law broke up my marriage. One day my wife came home early from work and found us in bed together.
— *Lenny Bruce*

She said he proposed something on their wedding night her own brother wouldn't have suggested.
— *James Thurber*

> *Love is a fever which marriage puts to bed.*
> — Richard Needham

Familiarity breeds contempt . . . and children.
— *Mark Twain*

With those delicate features of his, he would have made a pretty woman, and he probably never has.
— *Josefa Heifitz*

> *Sex is an emotion in motion.*
> — Mae West

I wish Adam had died with all his ribs in his body.
— *Dion Boucicault*

The trouble with some women is that they get all excited about nothing . . . and then marry him.
— *Cher*

Sexual Intellectual

It's the good girls who keep the diaries; the bad girls never have the time.
— *Tallulah Bankhead*

I was so naive as a kid I used to sneak behind the barn and do nothing. — *Johnny Carson*

> *What men desire is a virgin who is a whore.*
> — Edward Dahlberg

> *I was married by a judge. I should have asked for a jury.*
> — George Burns

If a diplomat says "yes," he means "maybe." If he says "maybe," he means "no." And if he says "no," he's no diplomat. If a lady says "no," she means "maybe." If she says "maybe," she means "yes." And if she says "yes," she's no lady.
— *Anonymous*

Sexual Intellectual

A man in love mistakes a pimple for a dimple.
— *Japanese proverb*

Love is an ocean of emotions entirely surrounded by expenses.
— *Sir James Dewar*

> *Every woman should marry — and no man.*
> — Benjamin Disraeli

Enjoy yourself. If you can't enjoy yourself, enjoy somebody else.
— *Jack Schaefer*

SEXUAL INTELLECTUAL

First love is a kind of vaccination which saves a man from catching the complaint a second time.

— Honoré de Balzac

SEXUAL INTELLECTUAL

Buy old masters. They bring better prices than young mistresses.
— *William Maxwell Aitken, Lord Beaverbrook*

> *Here's to our wives and sweethearts — may they never meet.*
> — *John Bunny*

Courtship to marriage is as a very witty prologue to a very dull play.
— *William Congreve*

I recommend masturbation because it's cheaper and you meet a better class of people that way.
— *Buddy Hackett*

SEXUAL INTELLECTUAL

Men are creatures with two legs and eight hands.
— *Jayne Mansfield*

SEXUAL INTELLECTUAL

It's relaxing to go out with my ex-wife because she already knows I'm an idiot.
— *Warren Thomas*

Can you imagine a world without men? No crime and lots of happy, fat women.
— *Sylvia*

One more drink and I'll be under the host.
— *Dorothy Parker*

It is possible that blondes also prefer gentlemen.
— *Mamie Van Doren*

SEXUAL INTELLECTUAL

> *The happiest liaisons are based on mutual misunderstanding.*
> — La Rochefoucauld

The one charm of marriage is that it makes a life of deception absolutely necessary for both parties.
— *Oscar Wilde*

Whether a pretty woman grants or withholds her favors, she always likes to be asked for them.
— *Ovid*

SEXUAL INTELLECTUAL

> Sometimes a cigar is just a cigar.
> — *Sigmund Freud*

> *Women have served all these centuries as looking glasses possessing the magic and delicious power of reflecting the figure of man at twice its natural size.*
> — Virginia Woolf

> *You are not permitted to kill a woman who has wronged you, but nothing forbids you to reflect that she is growing older every minute. You are avenged 1,440 times a day.*
> — Ambrose Bierce

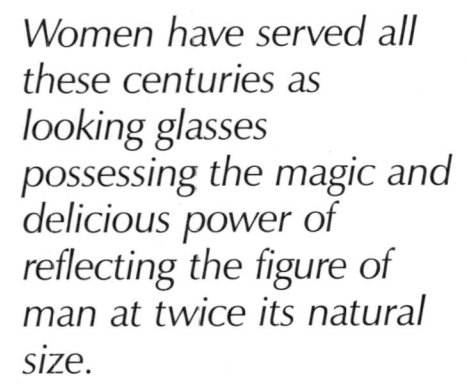

SEXUAL INTELLECTUAL

I've been in more laps than a napkin.
— *Mae West*

The kiss originated when the first male reptile licked the first female reptile, implying in a subtle, complimentary way that she was as succulent as the small reptile he had for dinner the night before.
— F. Scott Fitzgerald

As for that topsy-turvy known as soixante-neuf, personally I have always felt it to be madly confusing, like trying to pat your head and rub your stomach at the same time.
— Helen Lawrenson

SEXUAL INTELLECTUAL

Bigamy is having one wife too many. Monogamy is the same.
— *Oscar Wilde*

Here lies my wife: here let her lie! / Now she's at rest, and so am I.
— *John Dryden*

A good marriage would be between a blind wife and a deaf husband.
— *Michel de Montaigne*

Don't assume that every sad-eyed woman has loved and lost — she may have got him.
— *Anonymous*

SEXUAL INTELLECTUAL

Eighty percent of married men cheat in America. The rest cheat in Europe.

— *Jackie Mason*

SEXUAL INTELLECTUAL

When a man steals your wife, there is no better revenge than to let him keep her.
— *Sacha Guitry*

The difference between pornography and erotica is lighting.
— *Gloria Leonard*

My choice early in life was either to be a piano player in a whorehouse or a politician. And to tell the truth, there's hardly a difference.
— *Harry S. Truman*

SEXUAL INTELLECTUAL

The majority of husbands remind me of an orangutan trying to play the violin.
— *Honoré de Balzac*

SEXUAL INTELLECTUAL

A gentleman who had been very unhappy in marriage married immediately after his wife died; Johnson said it was the triumph of hope over experience.
— *James Boswell*

I'm too shy to express my sexual needs except over the phone to people I don't know.
— *Garry Shandling*

I married beneath me. All women do.
— Nancy, Lady Astor

SEXUAL INTELLECTUAL

One man's folly is another man's wife.
— *Helen Rowland*

> *The trouble with incest is that it gets you involved with relatives.*
> *— George S. Kaufman*

My wife and I tried to breakfast together, but we had to stop or our marriage would have been wrecked.
— *Sir Winston Spencer Churchill*

SEXUAL INTELLECTUAL

Marriage: a ceremony in which rings are put on the finger of the lady and through the nose of the gentleman.
— *Herbert Spencer*

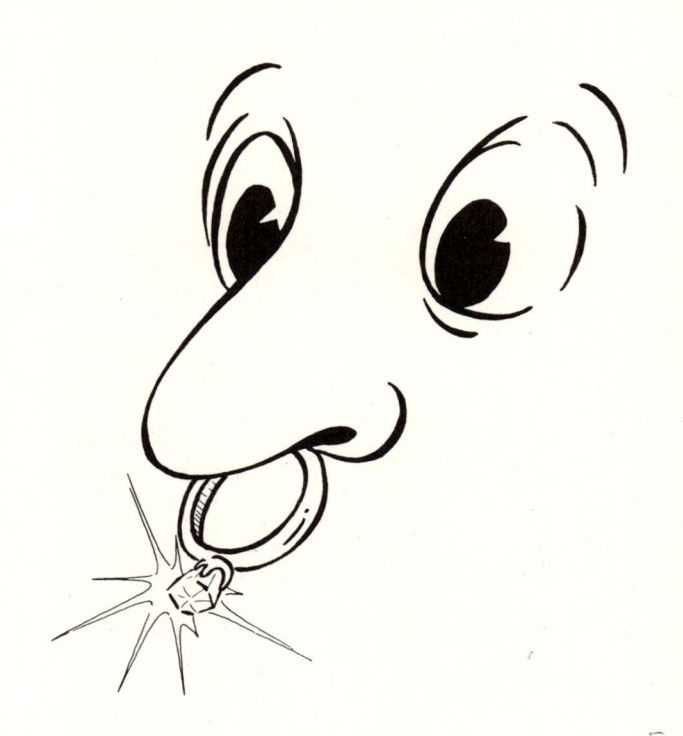

Love is the delusion that one woman differs from another.
— *H. L. Mencken*

Sex is nobody's business except the three people involved.
— Anonymous

Polygamy: an endeavor to get more out of life than there is in it.
— Elbert Hubbard

To enter life by way of the vagina is as good a way as any.
— *Henry Miller*

SEXUAL INTELLECTUAL

Bisexuality immediately doubles your chances for a date on Saturday night.
— *Woody Allen*

Someone once said that the Lord made the universe and rested. The Lord made man and rested. The Lord made woman — and since then neither the Lord nor man has rested.
 — *Lyndon Baines Johnson*

> *A man is already halfway in love with any woman who listens to him.*
> — Brendan Francis

SEXUAL INTELLECTUAL

Many a man has fallen in love with a girl in a light so dim that he would not have chosen a suit by it.
— *Maurice Chevalier*

SEXUAL INTELLECTUAL

She was so wild that when she made French toast, she got her tongue caught in the toaster.
— *Rodney Dangerfield*

I can't believe that out of 100,000 sperm, you were the quickest.
— *Steven Pearl*

A lady is one who never shows her underwear unintentionally.
— *Lillian Day*

> Her face was her chaperone.
> — Rupert Hughes

Anyone who says he can see through women is missing a lot.
— *Groucho Marx*

SEXUAL INTELLECTUAL

> What I like about masturbation is that you don't have to talk afterwards.
> — Milos Forman

A fox is a wolf who sends flowers.
— Ruth Weston

Marrying a man is like buying something you've been admiring for a long time in a shop window. You may love it when you get it home, but it doesn't always go with everything else in the house.
— Jean Kerr

SEXUAL INTELLECTUAL

Marriage is a lot like the army: Everyone complains, but you'd be surprised at the large number that reenlist.
— *James Garner*

His designs were strictly honorable, as the phrase is; that is, to rob a lady of her fortune by way of marriage.
— *Henry Fielding*

I kissed my first girl and smoked my first cigarette on the same day. I haven't had time for tobacco since.
— *Arturo Toscanini*

Sexual Intellectual

Marriage is like twirling a baton, turning handsprings or eating with chopsticks: It looks easy till you try it.

— *Anonymous*

A wife lasts only for the length of the marriage, but an ex-wife is there for the rest of your life.
— *Jim Samuels*

> *I have an intense desire to return to the womb. Anybody's.*
> — Woody Allen

He who falls in love with himself will have no rivals.
— *Anonymous*

Someday we'll look back on this moment and plow into a parked car.
— *Evan Davis*

SEXUAL INTELLECTUAL

The honeymoon is over when he phones to say he'll be late for supper and she's already left a note that it's in the refrigerator.
— *Bill Lawrence*

> *Women would rather be right than reasonable.*
> — Ogden Nash

Marriage is popular because it combines the maximum of temptation with the maximum of opportunity.
— *George Bernard Shaw*

SEXUAL INTELLECTUAL

The nightingale will run out of songs before a woman runs out of conversation.
— *Spanish proverb*

An archeologist is the best husband a woman can have; the older she gets the more interested he is in her.
— *Agatha Christie*

SEXUAL INTELLECTUAL

What is annoying about love is that it is a crime which one cannot do without an accomplice.
— *Charles Baudelaire*

> *It is not easy to be a pretty woman without causing mischief.*
> — *Anatole France*

Say goodbye to your best friend at a wedding reception . . . unless, of course, your best friend is of the opposite sex, in which case, you've married the wrong person.
— *Andrew Ward*

SEXUAL INTELLECTUAL

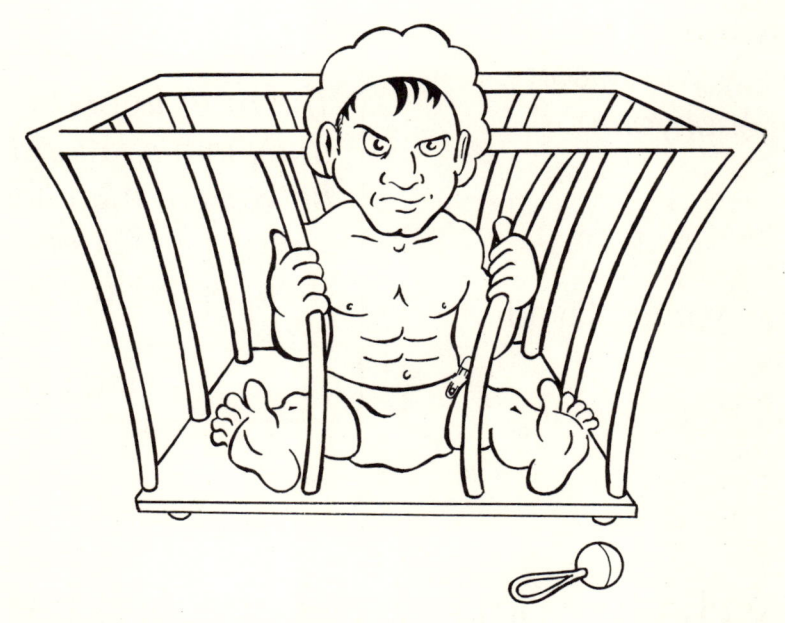

I like men to behave like men — strong and childish.
— Francoise Sagan

SEXUAL INTELLECTUAL

Vasectomy means never having to say you're sorry.
— *Anonyomous*

Divorce is a game played by lawyers.
— *Cary Grant*

> *The most important thing in a relationship between a man and a woman is that one of them be good at taking orders.*
> —Linda Festa

The only chaste woman is the one who has not been asked.
— *Spanish proverb*

SEXUAL INTELLECTUAL

If men could get pregnant, abortion would be a sacrament.
— *Florynce Kennedy*

SEXUAL INTELLECTUAL

Women, melons and cheese should be chosen by weight.
— *Spanish proverb*

Keep your eyes wide open before marriage; half shut afterwards.
— *Benjamin Franklin*

SEXUAL INTELLECTUAL

Husbands are like fires. They go out if unattended.
— Zsa Zsa Gabor

> *Love is not the dying moan of a distant violin — it's the triumphant twang of a bedspring.*
> *— S.J. Perelman*

> *The usual masculine disillusionment is discovering that a woman has a brain.*
> *— Margaret Mitchell*

Honesty has ruined more marriages than infidelity.
— *Charles McCabe*

SEXUAL INTELLECTUAL

The closest I ever came to a *ménage à trois* was once I dated a schizophrenic.
— *Rita Rudner*

I'd like to have a girl, and I'm saving my money so I can get a good one.
— *Bob Nickman*

She is a woman so beautiful that to expect sense from her would be hoggish.
— *William II of Germany*

SEXUAL INTELLECTUAL

I'm against group sex because I wouldn't know where to put my elbows.

— *Martin Cruz Smith*

SEXUAL INTELLECTUAL

It is better to copulate than never.
— *Robert Heinlein*

In various stages of her life, a woman resembles the continents of the world. From thirteen to eighteen, she's like Africa — virgin territory, unexplored; from eighteen to thirty, she's like Asia — hot and exotic; from thirty to forty-five, she's like America — fully explored and free with her resources; from forty-five to fifty-five, she's like Europe — exhausted, but not without places of interest; after fifty-five, she's like Australia — everybody knows it's down there but nobody much cares.
— *Al Boliska*

SEXUAL INTELLECTUAL

> *What's the worst portion in this mortal life?*
> *A pensive mistress, and a yelping wife.*
> — Theodore Roethke

It takes a woman twenty years to make a man of her son, and another woman twenty minutes to make a fool of him.
— *Helen Rowland*

Some marriages are made in heaven. But so are thunder and lightning.
— *Anonymous*

Sexual Intellectual

She looked as if butter wouldn't melt in her mouth — or anywhere else.
— Elsa Lanchester

It is now possible for a flight attendant to get a pilot pregnant.
— Richard J. Ferris

I'm through with men . . . I just want to be left alone with my vibrator. Yet another example of . . . men being replaced by their machines.
— Lisa Alther

Marriage is not a word but a sentence.
— **Anonymous**

SEXUAL INTELLECTUAL

> *A dress makes no sense unless it inspires men to want to take it off you.*
> — Francoise Sagan

One of the advantages of living alone is that you don't have to wake up in the arms of a loved one.
— *Marion Smith*

Many a man in love with a dimple makes the mistake of marrying the whole girl.
— *Stephen Leacock*

SEXUAL INTELLECTUAL

Marriage is the only war in which you sleep with the enemy.
— *Anonymous*

SEXUAL INTELLECTUAL

Fifty men outside? I'm tired. Send ten of them home.
— *Mae West*

> *Nature abhors a virgin — a frozen asset.*
> *— Clare Booth Luce*

The reason people sweat is so they won't catch fire when they make love.
— *Don Rose*

SEXUAL INTELLECTUAL

It is one of the superstitions of the human mind to have imagined that virginity could be a virtue.
— *Voltaire*

> *If love is the answer, could you rephrase the question?*
> — Lily Tomlin

Bachelors are providential beings; God created them for the consolation of widows and the hope of maids.
— *J. De Finod*

SEXUAL INTELLECTUAL

> *As a matter of biology, if something bites you it is probably female.*
> — Scott M. Kruse

> *If God wanted sex to be fun, He wouldn't have included children as punishment.*
> — Ed Bluestone

The fear of women is the basis of good health.
— *Spanish proverb*

There's one consolation about matrimony. When you look around you can always see somebody who did worse.
— *Warren H. Goldsmith*

SEXUAL INTELLECTUAL

Women want mediocre men, and men are working hard to be as mediocre as possible.
— *Margaret Meade*

> *Marriage could catch on again because living together is not quite living and not quite together. Premarital sex slowly evolves into premarital sox.*
> — Gerald Nachman

Sex appeal is fifty percent what you've got and fifty percent what people think you've got.
— *Sophia Loren*

Dave Pandres, Jr., has degrees in electrical engineering, math, and physics. He also has a sense of humor. He lives in Dahlonega, Georgia, where he is a professor of mathematics at North Georgia College.